YOU CAN'T WALK ON WATER IF YOU STAY IN THE BOAT

and more "RONdom Thoughts"

by RON BIRK

Golden Goat Publishers
San Marcos, Texas

Walk On!
Ron Birk

Also by Ron Birk:
What's A Nice God Like You Doing In A Place Like This?

YOU CAN'T WALK ON WATER IF YOU STAY IN THE BOAT

and more "RONdom Thoughts"

Library of Congress Catalog Card No. 93-091678

ISBN 0-9629331-1-2

Cover Artwork "The Plunge"
BY OTTER DREAMING
Jacket and Page Design
BY BARBARA J. MENCHACA

TABLE of CONTENTS

PREFACE

"I finished your book. Now I'm ready for the next one. When is it going to be published?"

These are the words every writer loves to hear. And fortunately I have been hearing many of you say that.

So here it is — more "RONdom Thoughts."

For those of you who may be new readers, "RONdom Thoughts" is a column I have been writing since 1980.

It started out as a feature in the monthly publication of the former Southern District of The American Lutheran Church. It continues today in *The Vista,* the official newspaper of the Southwestern Texas Synod of The Evangelical Lutheran Church in America.

In 1986 a weekly version of the column began to appear in community papers in Texas. That, too, continues in two publications, *The San Marcos Daily Record* and *The Mason County News.*

A collection of these columns was published in 1991 under the title *What's A Nice God Like You Doing In A Place Like This?* Reader response has been so good the book is now in its second printing. (If you have not read that book, there is an order blank at the back of this book.)

When people who are not familiar with my writings ask me to describe "RONdom Thoughts," I tell them it is a column of reflection and humor. In it I attempt to share things that have made me think and/or laugh.

Many of these thoughts come out of my own personal experiences. Events in my family life, or at our ranch, or while traveling — whatever, wherever — I am always looking for some happening or encounter that can be translated into a thought-provoking and/or smile-inducing piece of writing.

As a voracious reader, I am constantly stimulated by the random ruminations of other word merchants. That is another source of numerous columns. There are times when I like exactly what and how someone has said something. So I share it verbatim with my readers — always attempting to give proper credit to the original author.

On other occasions the ideas of another writer may spur me to take what they have begun and run with it. The result is something that is uniquely mine, but I owe someone else for the spark that kindled my creative fire.

That is the way creativity happens. It is a chain reaction. Your work inspires me. Mine moves someone else. His/her work, in turn, prompts another person's production. Etc. Etc. Etc.

Realizing that process, I want to thank all those who "turned on" my creative juices. If I consciously know who you are, I have given you credit. If I lost track of with whom my borrowed thoughts originated, hopefully they also have an understanding of this creative process. And therefore they will be gracious toward me and the way I used their ideas.

Which leads me to those of you who find "RONdom Thoughts" stimulating to your creativity. Go ahead and share your reflections upon my reflections, wherever, whenever, and with whomever you want. I understand and take pride and satisfaction in knowing I have been a part of the ever-continuing creative communication process.

And my thanks also to those of you whose gift is reading, not writing. Without you, we writers would be like actors without an audience, teachers without students, cooks without eaters.

Without readers, writers labor in vain. It is you sitting in your chair reading, that keeps me at my desk writing. Turning a blank sheet of paper into a page full of words is often a lonely, frustrating task. But when someone reads these words and is inspired, enlightened, or entertained by them, then all my toil is worthwhile. What you are doing right now as a reader affirms what I have been doing as a writer. And I appreciate it.

So, you read on. And I'll write on.

— Ron Birk

I have a confession to make.

Even though I am a fifth generation Texan, whenever I am asked my place of birth I must answer — Glendale, CALIFORNIA!

My parents, both native Texans, went to California in the late '20s to make their million. Instead they got the Depression and me!

They eventually came to their senses and moved back to Texas when I was five years old. But the damage was done. I will never be able to honestly wear a "Native Texan" T-shirt. I must be content with one that admits, "I Wasn't Born In Texas, But I Got Here As Quick As I Could!"

The first home I remember was near Corona, California, a small city east of Los Angeles, near Riverside. There my father owned what was known then as a "junk shop." Now it would be called an "antique" or "collectible" store.

We lived on a 10-acre "ranch" about two miles north of the store. It was mostly flat, clear pasture land with a few large eucalyptus trees around the modest frame house. I remember a small vineyard and a flock of chickens. But I can't recall other agricultural endeavors on my dad's part.

It was here I had my first pets. They were a small "feist terrier," named Zero, and his larger, part-collie companion, Tip.

The Corona home was the site of many weekend

get-togethers. My mother's two engraver brothers lived in Burbank and Pasadena. Regularly, Uncles Homer and Jack would bring their families to visit us and their parents, Grandpa and Grandma Williams, who had moved out from San Antonio and also lived on the ranch with us.

All in all, I have good memories of my two- to three-year tenure on that place.

It was 50 years before I went back to Corona. It was not that pleasant an experience.

I had one of my dad's old "Birk's House Of Bargains" business cards with the address, "510 Main Street." I thought that site would be simple to find. It wasn't.

In the intervening years, a freeway had been constructed right through downtown Corona. Now there are two "510 Mains." North and South. Both of them are in strip shopping centers. Nothing was familiar at all.

I had no address for the old ranch other than "Route 1." Still, I was able to follow latent memories and get in the general vicinity of my former home. Several times the "vibes" felt right, but I was never able to pinpoint the exact site.

My mind knew that chances were slim of finding anything as it was half a century before. So it accepted the fruitless search.

The gut, however, had been more hopeful, and was therefore more disappointed. Couldn't there have been just one little fragment left of my former connection to this place? Had all signs of my family's past presence been erased? Had the Birks and the Williams left no permanent mark on this community at all?

Maybe that is why my Texas home is so precious to me. It has been in the family nearly a hundred years. The ranch houses, barns, corrals, and other improvements have all been built by Birks. They either did it themselves or had it done according to their instructions.

Each member of my family has made a mark on this land. And even though changes to our ranch are continually being made, many of these signs from the past remain.

If my parents or grandparents were able to return from their graves for a visit, they would easily recognize the place. They would all find evidence of their previous presence.

I am determined to keep it that way. I have lost my first home. I don't intend to lose my second.

"I WISH I HAD WINGS LIKE A DOVE"

"I am worn out by my worries." That is the way the *Good News Bible* translates David's lament in the second verse of the 55th Psalm.

Stress and tension are obvious problems of contemporary society. And that cry of the Psalmist reminds us this is nothing new.

The struggle with stress has been around from the very beginning. I just imagine Eve had a few digestive problems after eating that forbidden fruit in the Garden of Eden.

And there were other biblical characters who found themselves in similar situations.

Think of the pressure old Noah must have felt trying to complete the ark and gather all those animals two-by-two before the rains began.

Or how about the tense muscles and sweaty palms little David must have experienced while walking out on that Palestinian plain to face the giant Goliath with only a slingshot.

Then there was Peter and the knot that surely must have appeared in his stomach when on that cool Jerusalem morning he heard the cock crow and realized he had denied Jesus three times.

And what of Christ himself? If Jesus was truly as human as we Christians teach and believe, he was not immune from the ravages of stress either.

In fact, the scene in the Garden of Gethsemane the night before his crucifixion seems to testify to that.

Mark writes, "Distress and anguish came over him, and he said to his disciples, 'The sorrow in my heart is so great that it almost crushes me.'" And Luke adds to the picture of tension when he writes, "In great anguish he prayed even more fervently; his sweat was like drops of blood falling to the ground."

No, stress and tension, pressure and worry, these are nothing new. Our biblical predecessors felt them as much as we do now. And their reaction to stress was also much the same as ours today — they wanted to escape it.

David cries out longingly in that 55th Psalm, "I wish I had wings like a dove. I would fly away and find rest. I would fly faraway and make my home in the desert. I would hurry and find myself a shelter from the raging wind and the storm."

Jesus had the same desire to run away from stress. And he did. Remember that scene in Mark 6 where we read, "There were so many people coming and going that Jesus and his disciples didn't even have time to eat. So he said to them, 'Let us go off by ourselves to some place where we will be alone and you can go rest awhile.' So they started out in a boat by themselves to a lonely place."

We pressure-ridden people of today can learn something from the example of Jesus. If he needed rest, then surely we do too.

Ford Motor Company has had a slogan, "The Best Never Rest." I understand what they are trying to get across in the context of that statement. But I think a more appropriate slogan for many of us today would be, "The Best Better Rest!"

Robert Orben has wisely observed, "The problem

with living life in the fast lane is — you get to the toll booth faster."

This ties in to Steven Wright's conclusion, "I think God's going to come down and pull civilization over for speeding."

But before he does, maybe some of us will be wise enough to slow down. Smart enough to get in our boats and go off by ourselves to a lonely place. Sensible enough to fly away on the wings of a dove and find rest.

SUNSET FOR SUNSET

"Sunset Carson, 63, a 1940s cowboy movie hero, died Tuesday of a heart attack in Reno, Nev."

That notice, tucked away in the "World Deaths" section of the newspaper, opened the curtains of memory in my mind. Out on the stage of nostalgia rode all the movie heroes of my childhood — Roy Rogers, Gene Autry, Rex Allen, Johnny Mack Brown, Allen "Rocky" Lane, Monte Hale, Lash LaRue, and Sunset Carson.

I was amazed that I remembered some of those names. They had flashed across the screen of my life over 45 years before. Some of them, like Sunset Carson, were only minor figures on the cinema range. They never achieved great fame or fortune like Roy and Gene. Yet they still played their part in contributing to the dreams of many a young boy.

Part of the Birk family ritual in the 1940s was to go to town on Saturdays. Along with my parents and grandparents, I would climb into the old Willys sedan, and off we would head for Brady.

Thirty rough and dusty dirt-road miles later, the paved streets of the "big city" would appear. We would enjoy their smoothness as they led us to the heart of the business district, "The Square."

After parking the car, we all went our separate ways. Older folks to do the weekly shopping and socializing, young Ronald to "The Picture Show."

There I would join a mob of other kids from Brady

and surrounding communities such as Fredonia, Voca, Camp San Saba, Calf Creek, Rochelle, Lohn, Melvin, and Pontotoc.

We would pay our 9¢ for a ticket, buy a 5¢ drink, some 1¢ candy, and enter into the dark, cool theater. There we sat enthralled through a double-feature and "selected short subjects."

In those years, B. T. (Before Television) and poor rural radio reception, this was a country boy's only exposure to the wonderful world of big time entertainment.

I remember few, if any, of the films of those years. Through their exposure in other mediums then and in years to come, I still have vivid impressions of Roy and Gene and Rex. But I am hard pressed to call up images of Rocky, Johnny Mack, Monte, Lash, and, least of all, Sunset.

The name sticks, as I'm sure some producer or agent meant it to. But what Sunset Carson looked like, what horse he rode, who his funny sidekick was, any distinguishing characteristics of his films — all are veiled by the clouds of time.

And yet, Sunset was one of those in the ranks of "influential people" in my life.

He met my need for entertainment and escape.

It got lonely being the only child on a remote ranch. Those Saturday heroes gave me something to look forward to, and something to take home. I would replay the last week's plot for the next several days as I rode my stick horse and, with my trusty cap pistol, protected our ranch from marauding bad guys.

Never once did we have cattle rustled, a water well poisoned, or a payroll robbed. I don't think my parents ever really appreciated what a good ranch security officer they had in their son.

Also, Sunset and his posse of pardners became inspirations to me. Not just to be a rootin', tootin', shootin' galloot like them, but to be an actor and entertainer.

All my years in front of radio microphones and television cameras, all my years standing in pulpits and on podiums, all my years sitting at a desk with pen in hand — all of these are the fruits of those seeds sown from the Saturday silver screen.

As Sunset Carson rode off into his final sunset, I hope somehow he knew that into at least one person's life he had brought a little sunshine.

"I CAN RESIST ANYTHING BUT . . . TEMPTATION"

For at least the past twenty years there has been a ruler on my desk inscribed with the words, "I can resist anything but — TEMPTATION!"

That famous quote from a character in Oscar Wilde's play "Lady Windemere's Fan" seems to catch the essence of a continuing dilemma in my life. Try as I may, I don't seem to have much success in resisting the temptations of which my life is so full.

I agree with the old limerick:

God's plan made a hopeful beginning
But man spoiled his chances by sinning.
We trust that the story
Will end in God's glory
But, at present, the other side's winning!

In my constant struggle with temptation I often feel like "the other side's winning." Even though I put up a valiant fight.

I identify with Andy Capp. In one of his cartoons, Andy is standing at a bar with a very attractive girl next to him. The girl turns to him and asks indignantly, "Are you trying to get fresh with me?" To which Andy replies, "No, Miss. I'm trying very hard *not* to!"

A glimmer of hope comes from a quote in *The Old Farmer's Almanac*: "Don't worry about avoiding temptation. As you grow older, it starts avoiding you!"

However, as I grow older I find that is not neces

sarily true. Temptation doesn't lessen, it just changes form.

Martin Luther was right when he observed that each age has its own peculiar temptations. "Young fellows are tempted by girls; men who are 30 years old are tempted by gold; when they are 40 years old they are tempted by honor and glory; and those who are 60 years old say to themselves, 'What a pious man I have become!'"

Temptation is with us always.

And temptation is with us all.

I used to think I was unique in this regard. But aging has brought the awareness that I am not that different after all. I am just like everybody else. All of us are tempted. All of us struggle. All of us fall.

We may have different weaknesses, but none of us has no weaknesses. Each of us has our "apple," our particular weakness that causes us to be susceptible to temptation.

Maybe therein lies the appeal of the Biblical account of Jesus' temptation in the wilderness. Here is something happening to Jesus with which we can each identify. We have been in that wilderness. We know what he was going through.

That may be the whole purpose of this incident in Jesus' life — for us to identify with him.

And for him to identify with us. In the wilderness Jesus identified with all of us who are constantly being tempted. The significance of that is spelled out in Hebrews 2:18, "Because he himself has suffered and been tempted, he is able to help those who are tempted."

Luther once said, "My temptation is this: that I think

I don't have a gracious God. . .It is the greatest grief. . .God hates it and he comforts us by saying, 'I am your God.'"

We do well to remember that Jesus was not left alone in his battle against temptation. The story of his struggle in the wilderness concludes, "Angels came and helped him."

Neither are we left alone in our tempted times. In our hours of trial divine reinforcements are with us.

We have that magnificent promise from Paul in 1 Corinthians 10:13, "God will not allow you to be tempted beyond your power to resist; but at the time you are tempted he will give you the strength to endure it, and so provide you with a way out."

Yes, there is temptation — but there is also power to resist.

Yes, there is evil — but there is also good.

Yes, there is Satan — but there are also "angels helping us."

God does not leave us in our wilderness, in our tempting time, alone. The Gospel is the promise that there is hope in the wilderness. No matter how barren and lonely, no matter how fearsome the wild beast, no matter how dark the prospects — God is with us!

As a result, I *can* resist anything, even temptation!

THERE'S GOOD GRAZING IN THE PASTURE

"Don't you ever feed your livestock?" Tex Luther almost had to holler to be heard over bawling cows, bleating goats, and a braying donkey. "Sounds like they are starving to death."

Tex had come along with me for a short visit at the ranch. As we drove up to the pens, animals came noisily running from every direction when they saw the pickup.

Now that we had stopped, cows lined the fence and goats milled about the truck. One old nanny goat even had her feet on the side of the door looking at Tex through the window with sad, hungry eyes. And Jacquie, the guard donkey, already had her head in an empty bucket in the back of the truck, rattling it around looking for one leftover kernel of corn.

"The cows were fed this morning," I said. "And you can see there's still plenty of protein blocks around for the goats. They're not starved. They're just spoiled. Every time they see the pickup, they think they're supposed to be fed."

Starting the motor, I eased my way through the goats and drove out to check the pastures.

Things looked gray and dry, but that's the way it's supposed to look in January in the Texas Hill Country. In fact, conditions were good enough for Tex to comment, "I don't know that much about ranching, but it looks to me like you've got quite a bit of grazing out here. Why do you feed at all?"

"It's supplemental feeding," I explained. "Give the goats some extra protein to help their mohair grow. The cows are calving, so they need a more balanced diet."

When we went back to the house and pens, here came the livestock again, eagerly anticipating some kind of handout. They proceeded to stay around the rest of the day as Tex and I messed around the house, barn, and sheds.

"Don't they ever go out in the pasture and eat?" Tex finally asked.

"Oh yeah, eventually," I said. "But they sure do waste a lot of time and energy hanging around here in between feeding times. They seem to forget this isn't the only place to get food. They get so dependent upon us to feed them, they forget to graze for themselves."

Tex smiled and said, "Reminds me of some church members I've had."

"How's that?"

"I think in every church where I've been pastor there were certain people who were there every time we opened the doors. They never missed an event. And they were there in between times, too. They would stop by my office several times a week to talk church business, ask religious questions, or discuss personal problems."

"You sound like that's bad," I said.

"No, not really," Tex replied. "It's hard to criticize people with such loyalty and dedication to their church. People with such a sincere hunger for what the church has to offer.

"I teach and believe," he continued, "that the church is the place to get fed good, nutritious, necessary soul food. So, I'm glad those folks are there."

"Then what's the problem?" I asked.

"Well, I'm just afraid people get so dependent on the church to feed them that they forget to graze for themselves. When Jesus said, 'Feed my sheep,' I don't think he meant that the church house is the only place to get that food. I believe there's a lot of 'good grazing in the pastures.' People need to come for regular 'feedings' at church events, sure. But they shouldn't forget there are other good sources of spiritual food where they came from."

"Such as?"

"Personal Bible study. Reading theological and inspirational books. Private prayer and meditation. Family devotions. Discussions with friends. Involvement in community service programs. Put all those things you get 'out in the pasture' together with what you get at the 'feed pen' of the church, and you have a good, balanced religious diet. Understand what I'm trying to say?"

"Yeah, I think so."

By then it was late and I was getting hungry. So I said, "Say, it's about time for supper. You want to eat at the house, or have a picnic out in the pasture?"

IF YOU CAN'T STOP ... DON'T START!"

In the mid-1940s my father, Willis Birk, and my uncle, Edwin Williams, started the Acme Brake Service in San Antonio. It was located on East Houston Street, not far from the Alamo. Even though the brake shop is now long gone, you can still see the site as you travel through downtown on IH-35.

The Acme (which, by the way, means "highest") was your typical small business. Nothing very exceptional or noteworthy about it — other than a catchy slogan: "If You Can't Stop — Don't Start!"

I admit I am prejudiced, but I still think that is one of the most appropriate commercial phrases I have ever heard. It states the significance of the brake business succinctly and provocatively.

The interesting thing about this little slogan is that it is appropriate for other businesses and professions as well. In fact, when I went into the ministry, or the "preaching business" as my father irreverently referred to it, he thought it applied there also.

"Before you get in the pulpit, Ronald," he would say with a twinkle in his eye, "be sure and remember, 'If You Can't Stop — Don't Start!'" That was his not too subtle way of reminding me of the importance of short sermons.

It has been good advice, not just in the pulpit, but from whatever podium I have found myself speaking. Being able to stop before you go too far is an important secret of success in the speaking profession.

That old business phrase also has other applications. When I was a rowdy teenager there would be occasions just before I went out on the town that my father would remind me of it.

"If You Can't Stop — Don't Start!" referred specifically to how I drove my 1939 Ford "hot-rod." But it didn't stop there. The way he said it, I realized he was making sly reference to my drinking and dating activities also. Hidden in those apparently superficial words, was a sincere concern for my well-being.

"Don't go too far, my son. Starting something you can't stop can have disastrous results. Not only can it wreck your pretty little green Ford, but it can royally mess up your life in many far-reaching ways. Your body, your mind, and your soul; your relationships with friends and family; your future health, finances, and career — all of these are dependent upon remembering 'If You Can't Stop — Don't Start!'"

That is still good advice. Follow it and all of us will prevent many wrecks in our lives.

Unfortunately, most of us are not as good as the advice we receive. Even though we know better, we *do* start a lot of things we can't stop. And as a result we often seem to end up in all kinds of collisions, from fender-benders to head-on smash-ups.

These tragic encounters leave us with various sorts of wounds and scars, from minor scratches and bruises, to major losses of physical and mental capacities. The consequences of ignoring the wisdom of "If You Can't Stop — Don't Start!" can be painful and dramatically life-changing.

Fortunately, we have parents and other persons in

our lives who live by the motto, "If You Start Loving Someone — You Don't Stop Loving Someone!" These are the people who not only give us advice, but who are also around when we don't follow that advice. The compassionate caretakers who are there to console us and help us pick up the pieces from our shattering encounters.

The slogan of the Acme Brake Service, "If You Can't Stop — Don't Start!" is wise counsel. But the motto of the Acme Caretakers Service, "If You Start — Don't Stop!" that is comforting good news.

DEATH IS A PART OF LIFE

Death has always been a part of my life.

Raised on a ranch, I became acquainted with death at an early age.

Animals would perish from illness or predators. They would also die from human hands. Pigs and calves were slaughtered. Chickens had their necks wrung. (Often by the most feminine of women folks.) All so we could have meat on the table.

Human death was no stranger to my childhood either. I regularly tagged along as my parents sat up with a neighbor's body. Funerals were community events. Everyone went. And we all filed by the open casket for one last look.

I was five when my first grandparent died. Thirty when my mother died. I was at her bedside and watched her take her last breath, as I did with my father almost 15 years later.

Professionally I have also lived closely with death.

As a campus pastor for 20 years working primarily with young adults, I did not have as many funerals as most of my parish peers. But when death did come to those with whom I ministered, it usually came in the form of tragedy.

A high school girl the victim of a hit and run driver as she and her date walked along the side of a street. A nine-month old infant riding in the back seat of her parents' car, alive one moment, dead from crib death the next. A couple returning from a fun weekend at the lake, a boat being pulled by a car coming toward them breaks loose, veers into their lane, plows into them head-on, and they are both killed instantly. A vibrant, talented middle-aged professor snuffed out by an aneurysm.

Death — I have seen it and thought about it, often.

Two thoughts seem to persist.

One regards my own eventual death.

Too often I think of death as "the sound of distant thunder at a picnic," to quote W. H. Auden. It is coming, but it is a long way off.

Like Robert Herhold, "Intellectually I know that I'm going to die, but emotionally I do not accept it.

"I keep thinking that something will intervene before my time comes, like the cavalry charging up in the last reel of a western movie."

I agree with Herhold, "It is important that emotionally I accept my death, so that I can get on with living. As long as I think that somehow I will be the exception, I deny my humanity. When I accept death, I join the rest of the mortals."

The second thought that emerges from my encounters with human death revolves around those words I have heard, and spoken myself, at so many funerals — "Christ died."

My religious faith has at its center the cross. It is a symbol of death, and a symbol of love.

Christ dying on the cross is the supreme expression of God's feeling toward we human beings. "For God loved the world so much that he gave his only Son, so that everyone who believes in him may not die but have eternal life."

Humans have long talked about making sacrifices to God. The unique twist of Christianity is that God makes a sacrifice for humans. Instead of us dying for God, he dies for us.

And in some miraculous, mysterious way, Christ's death is not only a sign of his love for me, his death also directly affects my death.

In the long sentence of life, the Divine Editor changes death from a period to a comma. As a result, no longer need I look toward death with dreadful expectation. Now I can look forward to it with hopeful anticipation.

Death has always been a part of life. But what Christ did on that Good Friday long ago, means that life will always be a part of death.

CAN CHILDREN AND ADULTS WORSHIP TOGETHER?

Some eyes turned, all ears tuned in, as the baby's wails echoed off the church walls and into the pews and pulpit, distracting the preacher in mid-sermon, and the worshippers in mid-worship.

As the frustrated parent struggled to quiet the crying child, various thoughts ran through the other churchgoers' minds:

Another parent — "Serves them right. Those were the same people who used to give me a hard time when my kid cried. Now maybe they'll understand."

Older worshipper — "Who says there aren't advantages to having bad ears. Turn this hearing aid down and I can worship in peace."

Another baby — "Hey, that sounds pretty good. And look at all the attention she's getting. I think I'll join in. Waaah!!!"

The preacher — "Hey, kid, this is a pretty good sermon you're disrupting. Where were you during last week's poorly prepared presentation? I would have welcomed any distraction then."

The child's parent — "O, Lord, get me through this situation and I'll never forget to use birth control again!"

There's an old story about a mother getting up to take her crying baby out of church. The pastor stops his sermon and says, "You don't have to take him out on my account. He's not bothering me."

The mother, not missing a stride, replies over her

shoulder, "Maybe so. But you're sure bothering him."

Children and worship — as long as the two have been around they have been giving each other problems.

There are certain rules of behavior expected in church that are, to be quite honest, totally unnatural for infants and small children.

Asking a baby not to cry is like asking a dog not to bark, a cat not to meow, a goat not to bleat. Babies cry — any time, any place, for any reason.

Small children are active, vocal, bundles of energy. Expecting them to be still and quiet for an hour is like expecting a ball not to bounce, a wave not to move, a bell not to ring.

Put a child into a normal worship setting and you can expect disruptions and distractions.

There will always be people who resent these young intruders who take away from their worship experience.

Worshippers have every right to expect their time in church to be a quiet interlude in hectic times; an uplifting experience in moments of depression; an encounter with God in an often ungodly world.

Worship leaders deserve to be listened to. Singers and musicians have spent long hours of training and practice to make a quality contribution to worship.

Preachers agonize in their studies getting just the right words, just the right illustrations, in just the right order, so that communication can take place and enlightenment and inspiration occur.

One loud howl, one dropped hymnal, one slow traipse to the bathroom — any of these momentary distractions can ruin the mood, break the communication process, waste the time and talents of those who have worked so hard to make this act of worship a meaningful experience.

Children and worship — are they compatible?

That is an age-old question with which the church has wrestled from the beginning of its existence. And yet totally satisfactory solutions to the dilemma seem to elude us.

Most Christians strongly believe that children are just as much a part of the church as adults. God loves both equally. Yet they have different needs, different expectations, in their relationship to God and the church.

How do we respect and minister to these differences? Can we really expect to totally gratify both adults and children at the same time, in the same place, as so many churches attempt to do in their regular Sunday worship services?

To be honest, I must admit I don't have a satisfactory solution to this dilemma. Do you?

THE SKINK IN THE SINK

I unlocked the door to the ranch house. Opened the windows. Went back outside to turn on the main water valve.

Then I returned to the kitchen to check and see if the water was running. It was.

So I began to rinse out the dust and other accumulations that had gathered in the sink since my last visit several days before.

As the water swirled around, I lifted the rubber mat to clean under it. Instinctively, I jumped back as a skink scurried out from its hiding place underneath.

We have a nice, friendly little family of these shiny, stubby-legged lizards around our ranch house. But this was the first time I had discovered one on the inside.

Evidently she had found a crack somewhere. Then got into the sink chasing an errant insect and couldn't get out because of the slick porcelain sides.

Recovering from my start, I easily caught the skink. She was then gently returned to her proper habitat, out of doors.

It was not many days after this that my wife and I were abruptly awakened at our San Marcos home in the middle of the night by an eerie sound. Something was scratching, fluttering, and lightly beating upon our bedroom window.

Getting up and opening the curtains, we could see the vague outline of spreading wings. I was fairly certain it wasn't an angel, but just to check, I turned on the light.

Taking a closer look, I found myself peering into the wide, staring eyes of a screech owl. He didn't seem scared of us at all. He just cocked his head and rolled his eyes at these strange night creatures that had disturbed his hunt.

When the owl didn't fly away, I tapped on the window. The tiny fowl fluttered his wings, but stayed put.

That led me to believe his talons were caught in the screen. So I thought I would open the window and help him out.

The sliding glass did it. The bird was scared away, flying back to his normal nighttime haunts.

The out-of-place owl and skink reminded me of the old saying, "A lot of things are easier to get into than out of."

How many of us have found ourselves in similar situations as the bird and the lizard?

It might have been a job that we took because it looked attractive on the surface. After a while, however, we regretted our decision as we discovered numerous noxious negatives about the position.

But by then we couldn't quit. Either the money, or the power, or the prestige of the position was too alluring to give up.

So we stayed on. Dreading to go to work in the morning. Drudging through the day. Dreaming of other things we would rather be doing. All the while unable to get out of a job that had us trapped like a skink in a sink.

Or maybe it was a "bad habit." At first we were drawn to it because of some gratifying sensation or beguiling sense of belonging — it made us feel good or a part of the crowd.

Soon, however, the darker side of what we were doing came to light — the unpleasant side-effects that made us feel bad and like an outcast.

But by then we were snared and couldn't stop. So we kept on furtively feeding our addiction. Suffering the torture of "the morning after." The twinges of guilt and remorse. The torment of sorrow and regret. All the while hooked on something we couldn't let go, like a screech owl on a screen.

If we were fortunate we managed somehow to survive these perilous situations. And, hopefully, we learned a lesson that will keep us from ever getting into the same situations again.

But if we are honest with ourselves, we know there are other "sinks" and "screens" out there just waiting to lure us into their deceptive depths and wily webs.

Some of these we will be able to resist because of the wisdom and wariness gained from our previous experiences. Others, however, will undoubtedly be successful in their seduction. Due to the weakness of our basic human nature we will succumb to their allure and once again find ourselves ensnared like the skink and the screech owl.

When that happens, as it surely will, our only hope is that there will be a helping hand available to lift us out of the sink, or scare us off the screen, with our skin unscarred and our feathers unruffled.

I DREAMED THERE WAS NO MUSIC

I had a dream. A terrible dream. I dreamed there was no music, that there never had been music.

In the dream I traveled through a sad, depressed, strangely silent world.

I walked through woods filled with birds, but empty of bird songs. The wind blew, but there was no murmuring breeze.

I went by men working in a town. They performed their tasks dully and deliberately. There was no happy humming. No carefree whistling. No spontaneous singing.

I entered a home. There were no pianos, no guitars, no harmonicas. There were no stereos, no portable radios, no stacks of tapes and CDs. From the nursery came no soft lullabies of a mother singing her baby to sleep. From the shower came no joyous sounds of a "bathroom baritone" greeting the day with a song.

In the yard of the home children were playing. But again something was missing. There were no happy groups playing "Ring Around The Rosy" or "London Bridge Is Falling Down." No solitary children entertaining themselves with nonsensical songs they had made up with their own words, their own tunes.

There was none of this — for there was no music.

Walking on, I talked to people. They had never heard of Beethoven, Bach, or Bernstein. Never heard of Frank Sinatra, Michael Jackson, or Willie Nelson.

Groups such as The Beatles, The Oak Ridge Boys, and Kiss had never existed.

I discovered that Americans had never stood proudly as they heard the stirring strains of "The Star Spangled Banner." Texans had never boisterously sung "The Eyes of Texas." Aggies had never stood stiff and misty-eyed as the nostalgic melody of "The Spirit Of Aggieland" drifted across a filled football stadium.

Continuing on my way, I came to the saddest place of all — a church.

It was Sunday. Standing outside the Sunday school building, it was depressingly quiet. From the open windows came no joyous voices singing with the exuberance of childhood, such oldies as "Jesus Loves Me" or "Come Into My Heart."

Entering the church building, I immediately *saw* things missing. There was no organ, no choir loft, no hymnals.

Sitting in a pew I opened a Bible. It, too, was changed. Whole books were missing. There were no *Psalms*. No *Song of Solomon*. David had never been king, because he had never played his harp and sung before Saul. Angels had been present at the birth of Jesus, but there were no heavenly voices singing "Glory to God in the Highest."

Then the worship began. There was no organ prelude. No choir processional. No opening hymn. No liturgy. No musical responses. No Psalmic invitation to "Come let us sing to the Lord; let us make a joyful noise to the rock of our salvation! Let us come into his presence with thanksgiving; let us make a joyful noise to him with songs of praise!"

There was none of this — because there was no music!

The silent church was too much. The terror of it all awakened me with a jolt.

Groggily sitting up in bed, I slowly became aware of birds singing. A radio was playing a pop tune. A neighbor was practicing her clarinet. Children were laughing and singing in a nearby playground. The breeze murmured through the trees. And from a distance I could hear the appealing peal of church bells.

It was only a dream. There *was* music in the world! And the world was a better place for it!

THE CROSS BRAND

Ranches have brands and earmarks. They are used as means of identification.

When I find a strange bull in one of my pastures, the first thing I look for is a brand. That symbol, burnt into his hide, tells me which of my several neighbors to contact about the wandering animal.

If goats that aren't mine join up with our herd, we look at their ears. A combination of cuts and slices in the ears, known in rancher jargon as "bits," "crops," "swallow-forks," etc., identifies the owner.

Livestock are known by their brands and earmarks. These show to whom they belong.

I branded my newest granddaughter recently.

No, I didn't stamp a hot iron to her backside. I baptized her.

As part of our Lutheran ritual, I made the sign of the cross on her forehead. This was accompanied with the words, "Bailey Marie Birk, child of God, you have been sealed by the Holy Spirit and marked with the cross of Christ forever."

In that act, as a worker on God's "ranch," I branded my granddaughter as a part of the Father's flock. She now has identity. She belongs.

She has the promise that "The Good Shepherd"

will care for her. If she accidentally strays from the "green pastures," he will go looking for her. If she intentionally crawls through the fence and runs away, God will keep the gate open for her, if and when she wants to return.

Bailey's brand means that she is marked for life as a child of God.

The sign of the cross, however, left no lasting impression upon her skin. The water of baptism quickly dried. In her four-month-old state of mind, Bailey had no idea of what happened to her.

Someday, someway, someone will have to communicate that to her.

And it is the other members of her flock who have that responsibility.

Those who feed her and read to her. Those who talk to her and walk with her. Those who care for her and share with her.

Mommy, daddy, sister. Grandparents, aunts, uncles. Baby sitters, day-care persons, teachers. Playmates, friends, and neighbors.

All who touch the life of Bailey are involved in the marking process. They call her attention to the brand. They tell her what it means to wear that mark. They show her the distinctive importance of that emblem.

This is not a one-day, one-way job. It is an on-going, life-long, multi-faceted process.

Bedtime prayers and table grace. Sunday school and worship. Vacation Bible school and church camp. Confirmation instruction and congregational youth group.

Personal words of guidance and encouragement —

"This is the way." "Thataway!" Timely gestures of understanding and support—a warm smile, a tender hug. Communal events of celebration and joy — a special family get-together, a significant church ceremony.

None of these alone is likely to get the message across. But put them all together at different ages and stages of her life, and little by little, piece by piece, slowly, but surely, Bailey will begin to put it all together.

Someday, if all the other members of the flock do their job, Bailey will be aware of her brand and the distinction that imprint brings with it. So when she asks the question everyone asks sooner or later — "Who am I?" — she will remember her baptism.

With that remembrance will come the assurance, the comfort, and the peace of realizing she has God's seal of approval.

Bailey Birk bears God's brand. She is a valuable resident of his ranch, and a cherished member of his family.

"WE PRAYED FOR HER"

"She's dead."

"I know. I heard. I'm sorry."

"She's dead. From cancer. And we prayed that she would be healed. We prayed fervently that she wouldn't die!"

"Yes, I know. I was one of those who joined with you in those prayers."

"Then what happened? You're a minister. Tell me why she died. Why our prayers weren't answered."

There was silence as the minister and the questioning friend looked into each other's eyes.

The brain of the minister was feverishly working to find the right response. One that was honest, yet compassionate. An answer that would not only speak to the mind, but to the heart as well.

This was not the time for glib cliches or shopworn answers from some dog-eared catechism on the shelf. This was a living, hurting soul sitting across from him craving some meaningful comfort and consolation.

Speak the wrong words and the hurt might be intensified and prolonged. Speak the right words. . .

"Maybe our prayers were answered," softly suggested the minister.

"What do you mean?" said the friend with a tinge of indignation in her voice.

"I mean, maybe death is a form of healing. We prayed because we didn't want her to suffer anymore. And now she isn't."

"I'm not sure I like, or agree with, what you're saying," replied the friend.

"I'm not sure I like it either," said the minister. "But I've been around too much death personally — both my parents died from long, lingering diseases — and professionally, to write off death as something automatically bad and evil.

"For many people there comes a time when for them to continue living in the condition they are in is just not good. Then death comes as a reliever of pain and misery. It comes as a welcome friend. It comes in answer to loving prayers for healing and relief."

The friend thought about this for a few minutes and then with tear-glistening eyes said, "But death seems like such a drastic cure. I didn't want her to die."

Weighing his words carefully, the minister reached out, took the sorrowing friend's hands into his and gently said, "I believe she is still alive."

"What?"

"I believe she is still alive. Jesus said, 'I am the resurrection and the life. Whoever believes in me will live, even though he dies; and whoever lives and believes in me *will never die!'*

"I believe she believed that," he said. "I believe Jesus keeps his promises. I believe she is still alive."

"I would like to believe that, too," said the friend. "But she died! We had a funeral and a burial. Explain how that fits with Jesus saying 'we will never die.'"

"I can't explain it," said the minister. "Other than it seems obvious we need to redefine some terms.

"We all know physical death takes place. We can't argue with that. But the biblical definition of death seems to be separation from God, while life means being with him. And we have that magnificent promise in Romans 8 that nothing can separate us from God, not even death. So if separation from God is death and there is nothing that can separate us from God — then we can never die!"

There was silence — a long silence. The friend seemed deep in thought. But the minister couldn't read her thoughts.

Had he said the right words?

A WARM HOUSE

It was a bitter, raw winter day in the Texas Hill Country. Somebody had left the gate open up in the Panhandle and a blue norther had escaped. As the blustery winds hit the center of the state, it soon became cold enough to freeze eggs on the sidewalk.

As I drove up to our ranch house after several days away, a shiver of anticipation ran up my spine. It was not due to the excitement of being back at the home place. It was because I knew what to expect when I walked into the house — cold!

And my expectations were met. Looking at the thermometer on the living-room table, I was not surprised to see a 26-degree reading. It was, as one of my friends had commented on a previous visit under the same conditions, "cold enough to hang meat in here!"

After turning on numerous gas and electric heaters and getting a roaring blaze going in the fireplace, the house soon became toasty and cozy. But still the initial chill that greets me on such winter visits is not that enjoyable.

Just the opposite happens, however, when I enter our house in town on such frigid days. The central-heated home welcomes me with warm arms. Walking into its rooms is a pleasurable experience. One I look forward to, not dread.

The contrast between the cool greeting in one house and the warm one in another, reminds me of other receptions I receive.

For example, as a professional speaker. There are times when I receive a very cold reception. Walking to the front of the audience, I can sense suspicion. "Who is this guy? I never heard of him. What does he know about our group? He's not from our area or profession. Why do I have to sit here and listen to him? I've got better things to do."

These are tough situations to deal with. It takes all of one's professionalism and communication skills to warm up such an audience. And, to be honest, it is not always a successful or fun experience.

On the other hand, walking into a room as a speaker and being met with familiar faces and hearty handshakes — few things are more delightful. Standing before this kind of crowd, I can feel the warmth and acceptance. "I have known Ron since we were in school together. I've heard him speak before. I've read his columns and his book. I count him as a friend. He's going to have something to say which will be provocative, yet amusing. I can hardly wait to hear him."

The difference between a warm and a cold initial reception as a speaker is almost always due to whether I am known by the audience or not. The better they know me — who I am, what I've done — the warmer they receive me. The less they know me, the cooler the welcome.

I have the feeling the difference between heaven and hell is much the same.

If one is unfortunate enough to end up in hell, I suspect that, in spite of the popular concept, one will receive a chilly reception.

Satan won't care who you are or where you came from. No one tending the furnaces will know your name. Your fellow pit-dwellers could care less about you. It may be hotter than blazes, but you're going to get the cold shoulder. And that just may be the worst thing about hell.

Heaven, on the other hand, will be a place where you are warmly received.

Peter will fling open the gates and greet you heartily, "Hey, Ron. Come on in. We've been expecting you!" God himself will rush off his throne, throw his arms around you in a big bear hug, and say, "Ron, my boy. Welcome home. I'm glad to see you!" And all the rest of the heavenly throng will come running and crowd around you smiling and hollering, "Ron's finally here. Boy, are we gonna have fun now. The party's complete!"

Now that is my idea of a warm house! I look forward to walking in there.

"What are you so excited about?"

"Boredom!"

"I'm sorry. I didn't understand you."

"Boredom. I'm excited about boredom!"

My conversations with friend Tex Luther often bordered on the strange, but this was a little weird even for him.

"Tex," I said, "please explain what you're talking about?"

"It's very simple," he replied. "I've been doing a lot of thinking lately about what's wrong with the church. Why many of the main-line denominations are losing members. And I'm excited because I think I may have finally come up with the answer."

"Which is?"

"Boredom!"

Seeing that I still did not understand what he was talking about, Tex went on.

"I ran across a statement by a Lutheran bishop who said, 'The besetting sin of the Lutheran Church is *not* poor theology, *not* poor structure, *not* untrained leaders. The problem is *boredom*. In a real sense the Lutheran Church has lost its soul. We know how to run the church, we know how to raise money, but we have lost the fire and fervor we need to make ours a vital force in society.'"

"That's exciting?" I asked.

"Yes," he said, "because it caused me to look further

into the subject. And I came up with others who have made the same observation."

"Such as?"

"Robert Short, for one. He wrote, 'Most Christian theology is not rejected because it is considered wrong. Few people get far enough into it to form this kind of opinion. It's simply rejected because it seems incomprehensible and boring.'

"And in his autobiographical work, *North Toward Home*," Tex continued, "writer Willie Morris comments on his waning relationship with the church by saying, 'With me the old-time religion began to wither not as a result of the exercise of brain cells, or the enlightenment of civilized discourse. . .but from plain human boredom.'

"Now do you understand what I'm talking about?"

Thinking a minute, I replied, "Yeah. You're saying the problem with the church is it has too many Bored-Again Christians!"

"Cute, Ron. Cute," said Tex. "But I'm serious. I think I'm on to something here."

He went on. "Soren Kierkegaard said, 'Boredom is the root of all evil.' And Bertrand Russell was saying much the same when he wrote, 'Boredom is a vital problem for the moralist, since at least half of the sins of mankind are caused by the fear of it.'"

"OK, Tex," I said, "I see your point. But, if you're going to quote quotes, what do you think of this one by Nietzsche? 'Against boredom, even the gods contend in vain.' Which caused author Kurt Vonnegut to conclude, 'We are supposed to be bored. It is a part of life. Learn to put up with it, or you will not be. . .mature women and men.'"

Smiling, Tex said, "I forgot. You collect quotes, too. But I disagree with yours. I think we must contend against boredom. We must fight against boredom being just another one of the crosses we have to bear in the church."

Warming to his subject, he continued, "Christianity is too exciting a religion to succumb to boredom. Can you imagine people being bored around Jesus? I just can't visualize any nodding heads during such miracles as the feeding of the 5,000 — or see any yawns among those gathered around the empty tomb on Easter morning.

"If I understand Christianity at all it is a 'Good News' religion—a chain-breaking, grave-opening, load-dumping religion. A religion that turns lives upside down! To make such an exciting and lively religion dull and boring has to be one of the greatest sins there is! Somehow, somehow we must battle boredom as the insidious threat it is to the church."

"Any suggestions?" I asked.

That question slowed Tex down, but only for a moment. "Well, I have to admit I'm still working on that," he said. "However, before you make some smart remark, just remember another old quote, 'A problem well defined, is a problem half solved.'"

THE SNAKES OF EDEN

Snakes! I don't like them.

As one who was raised in snake-laden country by a snake-hating father, I was taught at an early age, "The only good snake is a dead snake."

Rationally I know that is not true. Snakes have a very important role to play in our ecological system. Indiscriminately to kill snakes is to mess with the Master's master plan.

But emotionally I am more a child of my father on earth than my Father in heaven. I see a snake and my first reaction is, "Kill!"

In my old age I have mellowed and matured to the extent that I have gained a certain amount of control over my actions. At least I don't kill non-poisonous snakes anymore.

When it comes to rattlesnakes, however, I'm still my old self. They scare me. And I react to that fear by killing, or at least trying to kill, every one I see.

Regular encounters at the family ranch don't help to change that attitude.

For example, there was the time I was mowing weeds around an old rock tank so snakes could be seen more easily. All of a sudden, I start mowing a rattlesnake! Talk about a surprise to both of us! I go one way. The snake goes another. And the mower keeps going ahead on its own.

I quickly got my gun, but the snake had departed posthaste for higher grass and I never found him.

But his memory lingered on.

Then there was the time we were getting ready to shear goats. It was bright and early in the morning. We were separating goats in the pens when I heard the shivering shake of a snake's tail. (That'll wake you up faster than a whole pot of coffee!) Looking around I saw a rattlesnake about four-feet long coiled up in the corner of the goat shed. This time my gun was handy. Goodbye snake!

Another encounter was also during shearing time. I was making a last swing through the pasture looking for goats we might have missed. It was an exceptionally warm day for the last of February, and as I approached a known snake den area I was on the lookout for the creepy, crawly critters. Sure enough, I spotted one sunning. Quickly I sent him to snake heaven.

Looking around I saw another rattler. And another! And another! Bam! Bam! Bam! In a matter of a couple of minutes, in the space of about six square feet, I had killed four large rattlesnakes.

I consider our ranch my retreat place. My place to get away from all the cares and woes of my life. Yet in my idyllic paradise, it has not been unusual to kill from six to twelve rattling reptiles a year.

Why in every Garden of Eden does there always seem to be a serpent?

But the snakes don't keep me from enjoying my Eden. I remind myself that in the 90-something years the ranch has been in the Birk family, as far as I know, no one has ever been bitten by a rattlesnake, while literally hundreds of snakes have bitten the dust.

These are pretty good odds. So I keep going back. Keeping eyes and ears alert for signs of snakes, yes, but still enjoying my Eden and all its pleasures. No snake is going to run me out of my Garden!

Chances are you, too, have an Eden. Like mine, it may be a place. It may be a relationship, or a job, or a hobby. Your "paradise" can be anyone or anything that gives you great joy and pleasure, that makes your life worth living.

And again, like me, chances are your Eden has a "serpent." Some flaw that makes it less than perfect. But you don't let that "snake" run you out of the garden. It may be an unpleasant nuisance, but it is no reason to forsake all the pleasure of your "paradise."

The point of all this?

Let's enjoy our Edens — snakes and all!

YOU CAN'T WALK ON WATER IF YOU STAY IN THE BOAT

"There are two basic rules of life, " writes Roger Von Oech. "Number one: change is inevitable. Number two: everybody resists change."

Roy Blitzer underscores that observation when he says, "The only person who likes change is a wet baby."

Change is not that popular in the church either.

A speaker at a Lutheran pastors' conference told the story of a farmer back in the days before tractors. He had four mules named Baptist, Methodist, Episcopal, and Lutheran.

One day he was plowing and his neighbor heard him hollering out the mules' names.

"Why did you name those four mules after those religious denominations?" asked the neighbor.

"Because of their personalities," said the farmer. "For example: Ol' Baptist is hard to keep in the road. He's always wantin' to go off and wallow in the water holes. Ol' Methodist, you can hardly get him away from the barn. All he wants to do is hang around the feed trough. Ol' Episcopal, now there is one fancy, high-steppin' mule. And ol' Lutheran — well, ol' Lutheran won't go down no new road. No how! No way!"

Jesus may never change. He is the same "yesterday, today, and tomorrow." But it is an obvious reality that his church does change.

The church of today is not the same as it was when it came into being some 2000 years ago. It is not the same as it was in the 1500s during the Reformation. It is not the same as it was 100 years ago, or ten years ago, or even one year ago.

The philosophy, "You can't step in the same river twice," holds true for the church. It is always on the move. The church is constantly changing, always opening up new roads. And traveling them is risky, mainly because we don't know what is down those new roads.

But we won't know if we don't go!

There is a baseball philosophy that says, "You can't steal second-base with one foot on first-base."

We religious folks express the same truth when we say, "You can't walk on water if you stay in the boat."

Sure, something new is risky. Sure, something risky is scary. But Bruce Larson reminds us of a basic Christian truth when he writes, "Being saved has nothing to do with being safe."

There are times when Jesus calls us out of the security of the boat of routine and onto the stormy seas of change.

How we deal with that call will depend to a large degree on our attitude toward change.

For example: If you approach change with the philosophy of *Murphy's Law,* "If anything can go wrong, it will," chances are your expectations will be fulfilled. As someone has said, "Prophets of doom usually find doom."

On the other hand, if you approach change from the point of view of *Baughman's Law,* "If anything can go right, it might!" — chances are good that is exactly what is going to happen.

When Jesus calls us as individuals, or as a church, to climb over the side of the boat and put our trembling feet on the shaky sea of change, it takes a lot of courage, a lot of faith, to take that big step.

But when we do heed that call, trusting in Jesus' everpresent, supporting hand, we could just end up with an exhilarating ride on the waves! A ride that could lead us to the zestful crest of an adventurous new life!

OPPIE AND THE OPRY

"If Grandma Oppie could see me now!"

That was my first thought as I stood on the stage in Nashville in front of the microphone with the red-on-white inscription, "WSM—Grand Ole Opry."

One of my earliest memories of my Grandmother Birk was her sitting in her rocker in the ranch house, crocheting while listening to the music of Roy Acuff filtering through the static of the big old battery radio.

In many ways my grandmother was a fairly straight-laced lady. She didn't dance, or drink, or party. But she did like to read "True Confessions" magazine and listen to country music.

I suppose her love for the sounds of fiddle and banjo came from her heritage. Although Grandma was born in Texas, her Barrett and Barton ancestors came out of the hills of South Carolina and Georgia, bringing with them their tradition of mountain music.

As far as I know, Oppie never visited those old family states, never went to The Grand Ole Opry, never heard Roy Acuff or any other country music star in person. And yet I suspect she dreamed of them all.

So I think she would have been thrilled, and a little envious, to know that her only grandchild was doing all of those things.

These were the thoughts flitting through my mind

as I stood on the stage of The Grand Ole Opry — not as a performer (sad to say), but as a member of a special backstage tour.

Later the thoughts continued as I moved out into the auditorium and became a part of the audience, watching and listening, as many of my lifetime country music idols did perform on that stage.

Porter Waggoner, Charlie Walker, Skeeter Davis, Jack Greene, Bill Carlisle, Grandpa Jones — all did their thing.

Then the curtain dropped; there was a long pause, followed by the mellow voice of a WSM DJ announcing, "Ladies and gentlemen, the King of Country Music — Roy Acuff!"

As the curtain rose and that old familiar voice began to sing "The Wabash Cannonball," my skin started to tingle, my eyes grew moist, and my heart beat a little faster.

This was no recording broadcast from miles away, this was live, just a few rows in front of me.

"The Smoky Mountain Boys" showed off their talented fingers. Roy sang "The Great Speckled Bird." And then "the King" was joined by "the Queen" — Minnie Pearl!

The applause was deafening. There they were, two legends. Names known around the world. Faces that appear everywhere you turn in Nashville and Opryland. Stars with their own special museums right out the front door of The Grand Ole Opry.

As the two bantered away about Grinder's Switch and Cousin Billy Bob, the veil of nostalgia began to fall away, and reality set in.

I saw a tottering old man in his late eighties and a stooped lady in her seventies, fresh out of the hospital — two aging mortals whose days on the stage of life were dwindling down to a precious few.

The curtain came down on Grandma Oppie's life over 30 years ago. I knew it wouldn't be long before Roy and Minnie experienced the same.

But there was a time when these three were a team, whether they realized it or not.

The rocking lady on a remote Texas ranch, needles clicking, ear tuned to the radio, her life a little brighter, a little less lonely, because of the music that got her tired toes to tapping and the humor that put a smile on her sad face — Oppie needed The Opry.

And The Opry needed Oppie. Those big name entertainers miles away on the banks of Tennessee's Cumberland River were inspired and encouraged to share and sharpen their talents because of the acceptance, appreciation, and applause of audiences around America.

Oppie and The Opry — both would have been less without the other.

TWO SIDES OF HUNGER

The child
with bloated stomach
full of
hunger pains
and nausea
from too poor
and too little
food.
The man
with overhanging belly
full of
indigestion
and gas
from too rich
and too much
food.
They died in the same hospital.
The child
from
lack
of
food.
The man
from
too
much
food.

And Jesus said:
"Blessed
  are you
  that hunger
  for you
  shall be
  filled."
"Woe
  unto you
  that are full
  for you
  shall
  hunger."

ESCAPED GOATS

In goat-raising circles the story is told about the experiment once done at Texas A & M University. The researchers took three goats, put them into a large galvanized-steel tank, and welded it shut.

A week later the tank was opened. They found one goat dead. The second goat had stomach worms. And the third goat? It was gone!

That, for me, sums up the hazards of being in the goat business. And the biggest frustration of all is the constant battle with goats and fences.

When I was still a novice goat herder, I asked an old-timer in the profession, "What's the best kind of fence for goats?"

"Well, Ron," he said, "after years of trying about every kind of fencing known to mankind, I have finally come to the conclusion: if a fence won't hold water, it won't hold goats!"

My experience since then has proven my mentor's observation to be true. Hidden away somewhere deep inside every goat seems to be this dark urge to go under, over, or through any fence he/she encounters.

One personal experience will give you some idea of what I am talking about.

Deer had broken one wire in an 8-strand barbed wire fence. A nosy goat came along, saw the break, and decided to go through it. Other goats saw what was going on, and said, "Baa. Baa. Baa!" (Which translated means, "Say, that looks like fun. I want to do it, too!")

In short order **179** of our goats had gone through the small opening into our neighbor's pasture. But even then they were not satisfied. Traveling on to the next fence, they found another hole, and went through it into still another neighbor's pasture.

Finally the escapees were noticed, captured in a pen, and then freighted back to where they belonged.

The fence was quickly repaired. But there will be more broken and loose wires in the future. Will these, too, become goat gates? It just depends on who discovers the holes in the fence first, the gate keepers or the goat escapers.

The church title "pastor" comes from the Greek word for "shepherd." And many a ministerial shepherd has experienced the importance of regular fence mending when it comes to retaining church flocks.

In every congregation there seem to be some "goats" constantly on the lookout for the smallest "hole-in-the-fence" as an exit excuse. All the "wires" can be in place and in perfect shape. But let one "wire" break, and there is always the danger some member of the flock will see it as an opportunity to pack up and leave. And what is even more threatening, is to have other members follow, for no other reason than there is a "hole-in-the-fence" and someone else went through it. The herd instinct is not limited to the animal world.

The broken "wire" can be a significant matter of theology, church policy, or personal morality. More often, however, it is something simple like personality conflicts, misunderstood words/actions, or those seven deadliest words in the church, "We've never done it that way before!"

In any case, a break appears in the fence and members of the flock can use it as a way out.

Much more could be said about this constant hazard of the shepherding business. But suffice it to say, experienced and concerned pastors are regularly checking their fences. If wires are broken, they quickly mend them. And if members of the flock have already exited through the hole before it was discovered, good shepherds not only repair the fence, they go looking for the lost goats.

This fence mending is not a glamorous part of shepherding. It is not a fun part of shepherding. But I can guarantee you, it is a regular part of shepherding.

THE FATHER IN THE MIRROR

My dad has been dead since 1979. But I saw him this morning!

Head tilted forward emphasizing the dewlap under his chin, looking down at me over that slightly elongated nose with those distinctive Birk brown eyes — it was him all right. No question about it. There was the familiar face of my father in front of me.

I smiled as I recognized him. And he smiled back. Reflections have a tendency to do that.

Once again I had looked in the mirror and been amazed to see my dad looking back at me. For you see, the older I get, the more I look like my father.

And the more I act like him, too.

My wife, and others who knew my dad, regularly comment on our similar mannerisms. Gestures, facial expressions, body language — in all of these I reflect my father's influence.

In a very real sense I can say, "Whoever has seen me, has seen my father."

Realizing that basic truth about myself helps me understand what Jesus meant when he spoke the same words. When I look at Jesus, I get a good idea of who God, his Father, is.

The "Fatherhood of God" is a basic premise of the Christian faith. However, it is one of those things we hear so often that we may become dulled to what it really means.

To believe in a God who is a Father means basically two things.

One, it means we believe in a God who is Creator. God is the Father of all that is, especially we human beings.

This is not a uniquely Christian idea. We share this concept of God with many other religions.

However, there is a second aspect of our belief about God as Father which sets us apart from most other religions.

For us the term "Fatherhood of God" describes more than just a cold creator/creation relationship. It describes a warm, loving, caring, intimate father/child kinship between God and we human beings.

That is a significant difference. We believe God not only "fathered" us in the creation sense, he continues to "father" us in the best family sense of that word.

And where do we get this image of God? From his son, Jesus.

"The centre of the Christian conception of God," writes William Barclay, "is that he is like Jesus, that he is as kind, as loving, as merciful as Jesus was."

The prime role of Jesus in the divine scheme of things is to reflect God. Look at him and you see his Father.

But I am also a "child of God." That, too, is a basic Christian teaching. And a significant part of that belief is that I, and all of God's other children, reflect our Father. Look at us and you see God.

The big question is — when people look into our mirror, what kind of God, what kind of Father, do they see?

THE MIRROR OF MY SON

You know you're getting old when you can no longer cover your bald spot, even with the most creative combing.

You *really* know you're getting old, however, when you notice a bald spot on your son!

A Father's Day card I once received had on the front a picture of a young man in cap and sweater, with the words: "Dear Dad: Now that I've matured I'd like to take Father's Day as an opportunity to thank you for everything."

On the inside the card continues: "Everything but this, that is." And the young man doffs his cap and points to his balding head.

In previous pages I wrote about the experience of looking into the mirror and seeing the reflection of my father.

The other side of reflecting upon reflections is the experience of looking at my son and seeing me!

The idea of me being created in someone else's image is an emotional thought. But one that is not too hard for me to handle.

On the other hand, the realization that I have created someone in *my* image — that gets a little heavy. It brings up the whole subject of my influence upon, and my responsibility to, other people — especially my children.

I can't do a whole lot about the genetic heritage I pass on to my offspring. I give what I got.

My bald spot, and my son's, goes with being a part of the family. All our Birk ancestors that I knew, or have pictures of, were short of hair, too.

None of us chose to be bald ourselves, or for our children to be bald. That physical characteristic is a family trait passed on from one generation to the next, like it or not.

"The apple doesn't fall very far from the tree," is a proverbial way of stating this basic truth of life.

However, there is another old saying, "As the twig is bent, the tree will grow."

As a father I may not have any choice in the kind of tree that sprouts from my seed, but I can influence the shape that tree will eventually have.

The attitudes, emotions, and values of a child are usually determined by the parents more than anyone else.

Optimist or pessimist. Happy or sad. Loving or hateful. High or low self-esteem. Believer or unbeliever. This is where the reflection of the parent can often be seen in the child.

One winter day a man found it necessary to see a neighbor who lived beyond a steep and rugged mountain. He had climbed the dangerous trail for some time through the drifted snow and along the edge of a cliff when he heard a voice call: "Be careful, Daddy, I'm walking in your steps."

This is a cry every father, every mother, should never forget: "Be careful, I'm walking in your steps."

The influence our example has upon our children — and subsequently upon their children, and their children's children, and distant generations yet to come — cannot be emphasized enough. With parenthood comes a responsibility that has far-reaching, long lasting results.

That can be an awesome, scary thought. Or it can be looked upon as an exciting opportunity.

Not long after our son became a father himself, he came to visit. He had decided to give his wife a little vacation from the grind of motherhood. So he loaded up his 15-month-old daughter — and all the appropriate baggage that goes along with her — and came for a long weekend with Granny and Granddad.

As I watched him relate to his firstborn during those days, I was impressed. I saw sensitivity and patience, good cheer and pleasure, love and care. I saw our son doing a good job as a parent.

Then the realization hit me — that must mean *his* parents didn't do such a bad job, either!

And with grateful humility I remembered the Proverb, "A wise son makes a glad father." (10:1)

DO YOU SLEEP WELL ON STORMY NIGHTS?

It was one of those springtime thunderstorms that has a way of showing up unexpectedly during the wee hours of the morning.

As it approached the two Texas Hill Country ranches, the storm was courteous enough to announce its impending arrival with flashes of lightning and the rumble of thunder.

The two ranchers were instantly awake and aware of what was coming. After that, however, their individual reactions were totally different.

One immediately jumped out of bed and went into action.

The other, after a moment of thought, turned over, put his good ear into the pillow, his bad ear up, and promptly went back to sleep.

The awake rancher quickly put on his jeans and boots, and scurried around the house. He shut open windows and doors. The microwave oven was unplugged. He also pulled the plug on the TV and disconnected its antenna.

Then donning his hat, but shirtless, he ran outside.

First, he rolled up the car windows. Then he went to the pickup. There he took the tools he had been using the previous evening out of the uncovered bed of the truck and tossed them into the cab. He also made room up front for the open bucket of corn that had been in the back.

As the storm grew closer, the lightning became

brighter, the thunder louder, and the wind began to sway the trees.

Climbing into the pickup, the harried rancher quickly raised the windows. Then he started the truck and drove to the nearby goat pens.

His Angora goats had been sheared only a few weeks before, leaving them without their natural mohair-coat protection against cold and wet. Some of the females also had new babies. The goats needed shelter from the storm.

Most of the goats had sense enough to already be in the pens and under the shed. Others, especially the young kids, were scattered all over.

Frantically, as the first drops of rain began to hit his bare back, the rancher urged the reluctant flock under the shed. Picking up a couple of straggling kids, he finally got them all where they were supposed to be.

Then he dashed back to the truck, raced back to the house, and ran through the door just as the brunt of the storm hit.

Taking off his wet clothes, the rancher dried himself off with a towel. As he did so, he realized that he was just about as wet from sweat, as he was from rain.

Muttering a few choice words about his profession, he climbed back into bed.

Exhausted, but keyed up from his activities, the rancher couldn't go back to sleep. He just lay there, wide-eyed, listening to the fury of the storm.

His neighbor, meanwhile, was sleeping through the whole thing.

This rancher, you see, had listened to the evening weather report, which warned of possible thunderstorms.

Before going to bed, he had made sure his goats were under the shed. He had rolled up the windows on his vehicles and shut those in the house. He had unplugged and disconnected the TV and microwave. Then he had gone to sleep confident he was ready for whatever storms might come during the night.

During the short time he was awakened by the approaching storm, the sleepy rancher did a quick mental check to see if he had overlooked anything. Satisfied that everything was OK, he peacefully returned to his slumber.

Just before he drifted off, however, he remembered one of his dad's favorite sayings, "The more preparation, the less perspiration."

Do you sleep well on stormy nights?

THE PAVIOUR FOR THE SAVIOUR

There is an old English word that is still in our dictionaries, although seldom in our language. The word is "paviour." A paviour was one who paved a road, who "prepared the way," who made "paths straight."

John, the Baptizer, was a paviour. The paviour for the Saviour.

One way John paved the way for Jesus was by telling people to prepare for his coming.

If visitors are coming to our house we usually like to know. This gives us time to clean up the place and get things in order so we can be good hosts and not be embarrassed by a messy house.

John was telling the people that to prepare for the one who was coming they needed to "repent and be baptized." In essence he was saying, "Clean up your houses for the visit from the Holy One."

One way you do this is "to repent." "Repent" means lots of things, but a basic meaning is simply, self-awareness. To recognize and be willing to admit who and what you really are.

To be prepared to receive a Saviour from sin, one must see the need for such a Saviour. In short, you need to realize that you are a sinner before you can realize you need someone to save you from that sin.

That is not as easy as it may sound.

"Help me to admit I need help," could be a basic human prayer. Most of us are reluctant to face up to the fact of our weaknesses and shortcomings. It is painful and unpleasant to concede such harsh reality about ourselves.

Oftentimes someone else has to do that for us. So hardened are we against self-disclosure that sometimes it takes some sledge-hammer words to get through to us. And the wielder of the hammer is not always welcome. The person who forces us to see ourselves as we really are — no matter how truthful it is, no matter how beneficial it is for us in the long run — that person is usually not very popular. We just don't like to have our faults pointed out to us.

For example: Martin Luther was branded a heretic and an outlaw when he pointed out the flaws existent in the 16th century church.

Dietrich Bonhoefer and countless other confessing Christians were imprisoned and executed when they called attention to the demonic aspects of Nazi Germany.

Martin Luther King became one of the most hated men in America when he forced Americans to face up to the rampant racism that existed not only in our society, but in ourselves as well.

And John, the Baptizer, ended up with his head on a platter when he began to force the people of his day to own up to the unpleasant, sinful aspects of their lives.

Prophets are seldom popular. But prophets have been, and still remain, important parts of God's plan to prepare people to receive his Son.

Therefore, we might be doing ourselves a favor to listen to some of the 20th century voices crying in the wilderness. To open our ears to some of those unpopular prophets attempting to break down the walls we have built around ourselves, and thus open up a path for Christ so that he can come to us.

Who are these modern day John the Baptizers through whom God is trying to speak?

I'm not sure. But I suspect there may be some Johns among those strange, uncouth voices we hear and read about in news stories on TV and in the paper. These are the people who in their radical, unconventional ways are trying to shock us into awareness of what we are really doing to our world, to each other, and to ourselves.

We may not like these people. We may not like what they are saying. But that does not necessarily invalidate their message.

I have a sneaky, uneasy suspicion that I would not have liked John, the Baptizer. I'm uncomfortable around uncouth, unmannered, non-conformist, different, strange people. But I'm glad God sent John. I'm thankful John did and said what he did. I'm grateful for the role John played in preparing the way for Jesus.

So my prayer is that I may be open to whatever contemporary John the Baptizers there are floating around today. I pray that I may not cut them off without some sort of rational and objective hearing. For my own good, my own salvation, I pray that I remain open to hear what God has to say to me, no matter what kind of strange voices he may use.

I just realized I am beginning to sound like one of those strange voices myself. So let me quickly point out that God does not always speak through strange, negative, unpopular voices. Many times he uses very positive, lovable, prophetic voices to speak his words and prepare his way.

Mark Link has written, "Into the desert of our lives, there occasionally steps a John the Baptist — someone who speaks to us at a deeper level, someone who opens our eyes to something bigger than ourselves. It may be a friend, an inspiring teacher, or someone who radiates something more than ordinary people. Whoever it is, he points us toward a new star."

Who have been the Johns in your life? Who have been the paviours, the people who have paved the way for Christ to come into your life?

WE'RE ALL ON THIS RANCH TOGETHER

The dune buggy wouldn't start. That's not unusual. Left in a barn and only used occasionally, it is often reluctant to have its rest disturbed.

The battery was new and still sounded full of energy. So, I got out and went back to the exposed engine to see what I could see.

What I saw was — wires and tubes and hoses in mass disarray. Some were pulled loose, others lay on the ground, and some had been chewed in two.

Goats! Even though they had never bothered the dune buggy in the previous eight years it had been stored in this same place, for some reason this year the goats decided to add engine parts to their menu.

I proceeded to try and put things back in order. No luck. Realizing my mechanical limitations, I hooked up the tow bar, put the dead dune buggy behind the pickup, and headed for town and someone who knew more about these things than I.

Cruising down the road I recalled other animal escapades with ranch vehicles.

There was the time I was shredding a field and stopped to visit across the fence with a neighbor. While standing talking to him, a bunch of curious calves came to see what was going on.

I didn't think much about them milling around the tractor until I went back to start it. Nothing. Checking the engine I saw two of the four spark plug wires missing. One I discovered immediately on the ground below. The other I never found.

Fortunately, after rummaging around an old shed, my neighbor found an extra spark plug wire. Even though mis-matched, it worked and I was back on the row again.

And then there was the day my pickup was parked in front of the house and a crowd of steers came to gather around it. Watching them from the window of the house, I suddenly became aware of something I had never noticed before. There were little propellers on the sides of the truck, and the cattle were having a grand old time twirling them with their tongues.

On further inspection I discovered "the propellers" were actually the name-plates. The steers had licked them so hard the end brads had broken and now the plates spun easily on the remaining middle brad.

Ranch creatures do take their toll on ranch vehicles — and other things as well.

I've had dirt daubers make a nest in the exhaust pipe of a mower, so it wouldn't work. Owls have invaded deer blinds, leaving muck and mess 5-inches thick on the floor. Skunks have taken over an old storm cellar, polluting the surrounding air with emissions far above the EPA approved standard.

And even my bedroom is not safe. As I went to put on my boot one morning, I heard something rolling around inside. When I turned it upside down, out came a pecan that some enterprising mouse had stashed away for a late-night snack.

I could tell more such stories, but I think you get the point: Humans and other creatures who share the same space don't always agree on how that space, and items within it, are to be used.

I look at tractors and trucks as something to drive, not eat; hunting blinds as places of relaxation and recreation, not bird outhouses; and boots are made for walking, not rodent pantries.

Realistically, however, I've learned to look at the ranch and the human-made additions thereon from a non-human point of view and then plan accordingly.

If vehicle wires are tempting, park vehicles somewhere else. Blinds alluring, then have good window and door latches. A boot enticing, then always check before putting your foot in it.

Coexistence. That's the secret. Creatures and humans both have to make concessions when they share the same territory. The beasts and birds may have to change their eating, nesting, and storing habits a bit. The Homo sapiens change their parking, dressing, and security customs. But still they can live together, each doing their own thing without placing a great inconvenience upon the other.

And you know, somewhere in all this there just may be some insights on how humans of different opinions and lifestyles can share the same ranch — or house, or office, or neighborhood, or city, or state, or country, or planet.

Portraying a grandfather recovering from a heart attack, I was lying in bed in the Intensive Care Unit of Methodist Hospital in San Antonio. My "grandson" was visiting me. As the photographer went about his business, we were to carry on an ad-lib conversation.

G. W. Lee, a red-headed, freckle-faced, eight-year-old charmer, was my visitor. He listened to my heart through a stethoscope and watched the monitor, while I explained what happens when arteries get blocked.

Then I asked him what he had been doing, and he got to talking about his latest football game with his buddies.

During this time he was stretched out beside me on the bed, snuggled up under my arm.

Suddenly he twisted his head, looked into my eyes, and said, "Do you know what I want to be when I grow up?"

"No. What?"

"First, I want to be a football player. And then I want to be a granddad."

I must admit that being a grandfather was not among my career fantasies when I was eight years old — nor for a long, long time after that. However, now that I am one, I enjoy the role tremendously.

One of the highlights of the holiday season for me is the time I get to spend with my family. When the group gathers at the table I feel quite patriarchal. As

I look at, listen to, and enjoy the presence of these special people who are the direct and indirect "fruit of my loins," I especially relish the changes I have witnessed in their lives.

I look at a grandchild and remember her parent at that age. I look at my children relating to their children, and I try to recall how I related to them when I was at the same stage in my life.

This is a good awareness exercise in the cyclical aspects of history.

Another annual holiday event that always brings home to me how time brings change is an annual deer hunting excursion my son hosts for three of his buddies.

This is a group of guys who have been close friends since high school. For at least fifteen years, all or part of this gang have gathered at our ranch for a few days of chasing deer, eating hearty meals, and sharing intimate conversation.

Over the years I have become an honorary member of "The B Boys" (all their last names begin with the letter B), and it has been fun and enlightening to observe the changes as these carefree high school boys have evolved into rising young career and family men.

They now include a chemist, a college music instructor, a Texas Highway Patrolman on the Governor's Security Staff, and an executive with one of the world's largest record companies.

"The B Boys" still have a great, good time together, but where once they talked of girls, cars, and ambitions, now they speak of wives, homes, careers, and children, born or on the way.

Sitting on the sidelines observing these players in

their game of life reminds me of the same changes in my own life. As I once entertained my friends with my dad as a bemused onlooker, so someday my son will watch as his daughters and their friends play and mature.

People grow. People change. Today's grandchild is tomorrow's grandparent.

If grandchildren would remember that simple fact about who their grandparents once were, and if grandparents would remember who their grandchildren will one day be — maybe we would understand and appreciate each other just a little better.

THE DEMON FEAR

I was just a little tense. As I drove slowly up the dirt road to our ranch house, both hands gripped the steering wheel tighter than usual. My body was erect, almost stiff. Eyes searched the road ahead for any sign of human footprints.

Approaching the house and barns, I scanned every nook and cranny for human forms or movement.

Creeping to a halt in front of the house my heart beat a little faster. My seat gripped the car seat a little firmer. And my breaths became quicker and shorter.

Turning the motor off, I sat for several minutes looking for any sign of human intrusion.

The red dirt around the yard fence showed only goat hoof-prints. The gate was shut just like I had left it. Through the open windows everything looked normal.

Taking a deep breath, I got out of the van and slowly went up to the house. Sneaking one more careful look through the door, I cautiously entered.

Muscles tense, hairs on end, all senses alert, I checked things out. Nothing was disturbed. No one was there. No one had been there.

Sighing with relief, I took off my suit coat, loosened my tie, got a drink out of the refrigerator, and sat down to celebrate. The killer wasn't in my house!

I had just come from the Pontotoc Cemetery and the funeral of Hilton Herron. Hilton had been shot and killed in downtown Pontotoc just two days before, and his alleged killer was still on the loose somewhere in the vicinity.

The manhunt was being concentrated some five miles northeast of our ranch, but still no one seemed to know exactly where the object of the pursuit was.

I probably should have delayed my visit until the culprit was captured. However, with a bunch of high-priced cows and calves roaming the pastures, the water needed to be checked. And some goat kids being weaned needed to be fed.

Normally someone else does those chores for me. But that person is John Herron, Hilton's son. And right now he had other, more important, things on his mind.

Carefully considering the odds, I had figured chances were slim the fugitive was around our place, and had proceeded to drive in to check things out.

Finishing my drink, I put on some work clothes, got in the old ranch pickup, and quickly made my rounds. . .still with a wary eye and anxious gut.

In about an hour I was through. It was almost dark. Under normal circumstances I would have spent the night. But my wife had firmly expressed her opinion, "If they haven't caught that guy, don't you stay out there alone overnight!"

Again, normally, I would have resented her telling me what to do. This time, however, I didn't argue with her advice.

As I left the ranch and drove back to San Marcos, my anxiety level waned. But the subject of fear dominated my thinking.

The death of Hilton Herron was a horrible, tragic affair. It brought grief and sorrow to his family and friends. That was to be expected.

However, the widespread fear that pervaded the community while Hilton's killer remained uncaptured, with its effects upon our personal lives, that came as an unexpected, unpleasant surprise.

Doors were locked that hadn't been in years. Pickup gun racks were full. School bus routes were altered. Deliveries postponed. And I was not the only one staying away from his ranch.

"Fear is bondage," says an old English proverb. For three days in September of 1990 many of us in the area surrounding Pontotoc and Mason, Texas, were captives of that emotion. Our lives were altered by fear.

A Swedish proverb says, "Fear is greater than danger." The truth is, most of us were in no great danger during those days. But we didn't know that at the time. So we still experienced fear and all its negative effects.

How demonic! How destructive!

I don't have any glib answers to the problem of fear. But this experience has sharpened my awareness and increased my sensitivity toward those people around the world who live in communities and situations constantly dominated by the fear of real and imminent violence.

And that realization may be the one ray of light in the whole dark affair.

I DON'T UNDERSTAND GOD

"So many people who talk about God," writes Ashleigh Brilliant, "don't know what they are talking about."

That is true as far as this writer is concerned. I admit I don't understand God.

The reason why I don't understand God is very simple — he is God and I am human.

There is a lot of difference between these two.

For instance: I think in terms of time. God thinks in terms of eternity.

Everything I know and can comprehend has a beginning and an end; exists in a certain period of time; can be dated.

But God has no beginning, no end. He cannot be dated. He always has been, is now, and ever shall be. This I don't understand.

I am limited in space. God is not.

I cannot be in two places at once. It is impossible for me to be preaching from a pulpit and asleep on the back pew at the same time. I can only be in one place at one time.

But God is not so limited. God is everywhere all the time. He is with the orbiting astronaut, while at the same time he is with the coal miner a mile under the earth. He is with me as I write these words, and at the same time he is with my daughter a thousand miles away in Florida. This I don't understand.

I am always ready to hate and slow to forgive. God

is always ready to love and eager to forgive.

Somebody does something to me — hurts my body, my pride, or my property — and my natural tendency is to get mad and try to get even in some way. I will hold a grudge for a long time, because I don't forget so easy.

However, when someone does something to God — rubs his name in the dirt, flauntingly goes against his wishes, messes up his creation — his reaction is to hate the act, but still love the person. Forgiveness is immediately available. The incident is completely forgotten. No grudge, no punishment is held by God against the person he has forgiven. This I don't understand.

I am inclined to judge according to material values. God judges according to spiritual values.

I get rich. I am successful. I have my health. And I think this is good. This is all I need in life.

God allows my money to be lost. My success to dwindle. My health to fade. And he says this is good. That it is blessed to be poor and meek and weak. This I don't understand.

And there are many more things about God which I don't understand.

I don't understand how God made the universe. Or why he made humans.

I don't understand why he allowed humans to sin. Or why he thought enough of them to try to save them. Or why he chose the way of Christ and the cross to work out this salvation.

I don't understand how Christ rose from the dead. Or how God is with us today through his Holy Spirit.

I don't understand any of these things about God. And that is understandable. Because as Isaiah quotes the

Lord, "For my thoughts are not your thoughts, neither are your ways my ways. For as the heavens are higher than the earth, so are my ways higher than your ways, and my thoughts than your thoughts." (55:8, 9)

God by definition cannot be defined.

Fortunately it is a truth of life that reality is not dependent upon definition or comprehension. I don't have to understand something for it to be true.

I don't understand life. But I am still alive.

I don't understand light. But there is still a sun.

I don't understand love. But my family and friends still love me.

I don't understand God. But. . . . .

RON'S WRY RULES REGARDING RELIGION

After years of research and observation I have discovered certain natural laws that seem to exist within the church. Here are some of them:

★

The later you come to worship, the closer you sit to the front.

★

The earlier the worship service, the deadlier the singing.

★

No sermon is so orthodox that some hearer won't think it unorthodox.

★

The shorter the preparation, the longer the sermon.

★

The lesser the activity of a church member, the greater the criticism.

★

The poorer the preacher's preparation on a particular subject, the more likely there will be an authority on that subject in the audience.

★

The more announcements in the bulletin, the less they are read.

★

The more closed the mind, the more open the mouth.

★

There are Christian beliefs. There are things Christians believe. They are not always the same.

★

The popularity of a hymn is due more to the tune than to the words.

★

The earlier you come to worship to get a good seat, the more good seats there will be left after the service begins.

★

Emergencies will not arise until the minister has left his/her office.

★

Give a child a bulletin and he/she will draw pictures on it.

★

No sermon is as good (or as bad) as the preacher thinks it is.

★

In an air-conditioned church the number of men who are too warm will be equal to the number of women who are too cool.

★

If children get up to go to the rest room during the worship service it will always be just as the preacher reaches the climactic point of his/her sermon.

★

Just because people know the Ten Commandments is no sign they will keep the Ten Commandments.

★

No matter what the preacher says in his/her sermon there will always be someone who heard him/her say something different.

★

The more popular a preacher becomes, the more his/her peers suspect his/her theology.

★

If written and spoken correctly, theology is perfectly incomprehensible.

FROM PEN TO PEN

Put a shearing rig in the middle of a 25 x 25 foot enclosure; surround it with seven shearers, another couple of guys to pick up and bag the fresh shorn mohair; and then turn in 50 to 60 Angora goats at a time — and you have one dirty, noisy, crowded place.

There is the roar of the generator that powers the clickety-clickety of the clippers; the bleating of frightened goats; and bilingual voices raised loud enough to be heard over the clamor.

The wettest of earth soon can be turned into the driest dust by the milling hooves. The dust joins the fine mist of hair clippings to settle on anyone or anything in the vicinity. This mixture can seep deep into eyes, ears, and nostrils, remaining there for days.

A shearing pen is not a pretty or peaceful place. But it is a place to ponder.

As I leaned on the fence watching the activity in the goat pen, thoughts began to form that would eventually find their outlet in another pen — my writing pen.

I thought of the contrast between the shorn and unshorn goats crowded next to each other.

An Angora goat in full winter coat is a noble, fine figure of an animal. On the other hand, a naked goat is a pitiful, scrawny, sorry-looking sight.

A goat covered with its protective natural blanket can graze comfortably in open range during snow and sub-freezing temperature. While at the slightest sign of cool or wet weather, a freshly shorn goat will head for the shed, hunker up and shiver.

It's not all bad, however, for a goat to be out of its mohair. The danger of getting caught in briars and thorn bushes is gone. Some young goats can even get rear feet caught in their long, dangling belly hair. When this happens, they will often fall down, and then be unable to get up without human assistance. Shorn goats are freed from these hazards.

Thinking of this reminded me that there are also pros and cons to every situation in which we human beings find ourselves. Happy is the person who realizes this and looks for the positive side: who with St. Paul can say, "I have learned, in whatever state I am, to be content." (Phil. 4:11)

Next my thoughts went from the goats to the men working with them in the pen.

It has been said, "If it's worth doing, it's worth hiring someone who knows how to do it." I don't know how to do everything that needs doing on my ranch. That's why I hire people to shear my goats. They know what they're doing. They're pros.

E. B. White once observed, "I'd rather watch a gifted plumber than listen to a bad poet." That's my feeling about watching skilled shearers. It is a joy to behold them as they quickly and efficiently go about their work.

Many of these men may not be what the world would call educated, but they know their craft and they do it well. They provide a needed service. And I am grateful to them for that.

These thoughts vividly reminded me that goat-raising is a team sport. I am not in this alone. I am dependent upon a lot of other people, like the shearers, for whatever success I have.

For example: I have these goats today because my grandfather put together the original herd some 75 years ago. Then my dad took his turn taking care of the goats, and teaching me eventually to do the same.

Others currently on the goat team include: the breeders of the billies who help me continually upgrade the quality of the flock; the distant farmers who raise feed; and the mills and the stores that prepare and sell that feed.

Then there are: the research scientists who develop medicine and sprays to fight internal and external parasites; the workers who help me feed and doctor the goats; the warehousemen who store the clip; and ultimately, the buyers who purchase the mohair and send it, literally, around the world.

All of these people are partners in the process of helping me put mohair on the backs of my goats, and then getting it from there to the backs of human beings.

The more I think about it, the more I realize we are all partners on a larger scale. We all need each other not only in the goat business, but also as we go-at this business called life.

BEST FRIENDS:

THEY COME AND THEY GO

My best friend died recently.

It was an untimely death. He was 56 years old, at the peak of his professional life, a creative, caring campus pastor, respected and loved by many.

My best friend had been one of the most alive people I have ever known. That made his dying even harder for me to accept. I knew the illness was serious, but with his vitality, plus all the miracles of modern medicine, death seemed the remotest of possibilities. The news that he was gone hit me like a kick in the groin.

It is always tough to lose a friend, especially someone you called "best" friend. That four-letter adjective sets the person apart from all your other acquaintances. It means you have a special, intimate relationship with them like you have with no one else.

"Best" friends are people with whom you feel comfortable. You enjoy their company. Being with them makes you feel good. They become trusted confessors to whom you can open up and share thoughts and feelings, hopes and fears, dreams and regrets.

My best friend was such a person. For some ten years we shared the ups and downs of mutual careers, the pain and pride of parenthood, the waxing and waning of faith.

My sadness is that those years did not include

the time just prior to his death. We were still friends, but the intimacy, the closeness, the sharing had faded. The term "best friend" just didn't fit anymore.

The drift apart had begun some nine years before when I changed careers. The rift became wider upon his divorce and remarriage. We were not together as much as we once had been. And when we were, we didn't have that much in common as we had had before.

This is my first "best" friend to die. But he is not the first "best" friend to come and go in my life.

As I review my life I can count at least seven people who at one time or another I considered to be my "best" friends. (That does not include parents, wife, or children.) Some were neighbors or classmates. Others were co-workers or fellow professionals. And there were those with whom I shared mutual social or organizational interests.

None of these relationships ended with a bang. All just slowly faded away. We gradually moved apart. Sometimes physically. Sometimes mentally or emotionally. "Best friends" became "close friends." Then "friends." And finally "former friends."

This used to bother me. It made me feel guilty that I had done something wrong to destroy a relationship that had once flourished. But with the wisdom of aging I began to realize this is the rhythm of life. Times change. People change. Relationships change.

I have learned to accept that as a fact of life. So now, instead of regretting the "best" friends I have lost, I celebrate the "best" friends I once had.

I treasure the pleasure, the support, the growth that

all my "best" friends have contributed to my life. I am a different person, a better human being, because of our years of "best" friendship.

The death of a "best" friend reminds me to be thankful for all the "best" friends of my past. And to look forward with eager anticipation to all my new "best" friends of the future.

IN A BLIND, I SEE

I stealthily slipped up to the hunting blind, trying carefully not to disturb any whitetail deer that might be in the vicinity. Just as I went to open the door I caught a movement out of the corner of my eye.

Glancing up, I saw a goat looking at me from a nearby liveoak thicket. By the time I got inside the blind, that old nanny was right outside, plus about a hundred more that had been grazing hidden in the trees. They thought I had come to bring them some corn. So they had hurried over for a handout.

At first their uninvited presence perturbed me. It was too late in the afternoon to move to another blind. But then I thought, "What the heck. Their scent ought to mask mine. Let's just see what comes by."

As I settled in the chair, the goats began to lay down around the blind. Solemnly they chewed their cuds, waiting for me to eventually come out and share with them the corn they were sure I had.

It wasn't 15 minutes later that another movement caught my attention. Looking up, I saw a flock of over a dozen wild turkeys grazing right toward the goats, the blind, and me.

We don't have many turkeys and this was the first time any had been seen on our place during the first month of the season. So I was surprised at their presence.

I sat stone still as they filed by. The thought briefly crossed my mind, "Shoot one." But I wasn't really hungry for turkey — Thanksgiving was just over — and I was more enthralled in watching this rare passing parade without disturbing it.

I couldn't recall ever being this close to this many wild turkeys. It was a rare thrill to watch them peck seeds, pounce on insects, and preen feathers while totally unaware of my presence.

The scene was like something from a "National Geographic Special." However, instead of watching it on TV in my living room, this was a live production on the stage of my ranch with me in a front row seat.

The flock moved on and was out of sight within five minutes. But they left behind one happy hunter, who began to remember other rare blind encounters with creatures of the wild:

A half-grown bobcat playing with a freshly killed mouse; a pair of gray foxes coming out for their evening sojourn with the female diligently looking for prey and the male nonchalantly marking the boundaries of their territory with his scent; a curious squirrel coming down a nearby tree limb to within inches of the blind window to stare eyeball-to-eyeball with this two-legged animal in his cozy burrow; a huge ebony raven landing on the tin roof and entertaining me with a "do-si-do" from his talon-ted feet — all of these one-of-a-kind events, combined with who knows how many eye-opening sunrises and mind-boggling sunsets, have made for some memorable times in these small 4' x 4' outposts of silence and solitude.

As a result, I look forward to my hunting blind time with great expectations. I never know what I am going to see or experience.

The same holds true in regard to the mental, emotional, and spiritual surprises that await me.

In these restful retreats, these hidden hermitages, these mini-monasteries camouflaged as hunting blinds, I have had rare encounters with God and self.

Insights and revelations have come by as I sit still and quiet in a blind that I would never see if I were out and about. The hustle and bustle would scare them away.

Decisions about careers, awareness of meaningful relationships, creative ideas for writings and speeches — these are just a few of the paraders past my hunting blinds.

You may not be a deer hunter like me. But if you are a typical human being I suspect you are hunting for something — hope, peace, acceptance, purpose, whatever.

On your hunting trips after such elusive "game" don't overlook the importance of a "blind."

PRESS PASS TO PARADISE

Over 30,000 people crammed into the San Antonio Convention Center. They were there for the 1992 Biennial Convention of the American Association of Retired Persons.

Attracted by the ambience of the host city and an all-star array of speakers, the number of conventioneers far exceeded planners' expectations. The number was twice as many as those attending the previous convention in Orlando, Florida.

The result was mass chaos, as the huge number of registrants vied to get into meeting rooms that had limited seating of 4,000 or less. The AARPers were eager to hear such headliners as Barbara Bush, Bill Clinton, Ed Bradley, Lee Iacocca, Lady Bird Johnson, Shirley Chisholm, Ralph Nader, Liz Carpenter, Henry Cisneros, Louis Rukeyser, Dr. Joyce Brothers, Hugh Downs, Howard K. Smith, Dr. Art Ulene, Charles Osgood, Mark Russell, Irving R. Levine, Debbie Reynolds, and a host of other significant presenters, only a little less well known.

In spite of the crowds, I was able to get into every session I wanted to attend. As others lined up outside closed doors and beseeched the ushers to let them in, all to no avail, I would walk through the line and up to the entrance. There the attendant, with a quick glance at my name tag, would open the door and let me in, no questions asked.

The reason I received such privileged treatment

was not because of the name "Ron Birk" on my badge. It was because of a little orange ribbon hanging down from it, and the magical word printed thereon: "PRESS."

I was covering the convention as an on-camera reporter for Nostalgia Television, a national cable network. As a part of the working press, I had my run of the convention. I could go any place, anytime, with only a minimum of restrictions.

Talk about a feeling of power! But before my head swelled up and my britches got too big, a little inner voice whispered, "Remember, Ron, you're not getting all this special treatment because of who you are. It's because of who you're with."

That thought kept me semi-humble. It caused me to realize there was a religious analogy knocking around somewhere in this whole experience.

And it was: When I walk up to the pearly gates of heaven on Judgment Day, St. Peter will glance at my name tag, and immediately fling open the gates and wave me in with a welcoming smile!

Just as it was at the AARP convention, I will not be let in because of the "Ron Birk" on my badge. It will be because of a ribbon attached to my name tag inscribed with the words, "CHILD OF GOD." That will be enough to allow me to enter into all the privileges of paradise.

How do I get that pass into heaven? The same way I received my AARP press pass — not because of who I am, but who I'm with.

You and I have been chosen by Jesus to be in his family. Identified as a part of that team, we have access to all the inner sanctums of his kingdom. Nobody can keep us out. Nobody wants to keep us out. All the hosts of heaven will be delighted to welcome us in. They will take great pleasure in our enjoyment at rubbing shoulders with the headliners of history.

As a part of Jesus' "press corps" you and I are among the "in crowd." We are somebodies. Important somebodies. We can wear Christ's ribbon of identification with pride and honor.

I don't know about you, but I find that exciting. In fact, it makes me look forward with eager anticipation to that great "convention in the sky," and the day I can use my "press pass to paradise."

As the ranch father worked, riding the tractor, feeding the cattle, and repairing the fences, his young son played in the sand with his toy trucks, threw rocks off the hillside, and sat under the shade of an oak tree marveling at the red ants and their intricate "road" system branching out in various directions from the central bed.

As the boy grew into youth, the father eased him into the ranch work. The teenager helped round up goats and cattle, riding his horse where and when his father told him. In the corrals the son caught and wrestled down the calves, while the dad wielded the pocket knife. In ranch repair jobs, the youth provided the assisting extra pair of hands, while the father did the actual sawing, hammering, or bolting.

Time passed. The son grew into a young man. He went off to school, got married, began a career. He still frequented the family ranch, using it as a getaway place from the routine of his other life.

On his visits the son would take long walks through the hills and canyons, enjoying the panoramic vistas, the wide variety of wild life, and the scampering young calves and goat kids. In the evenings he would sit on the porch, or before the fireplace, soaking up the serenity of being away from the pressures and responsibilities of his job.

During these years the father was still in charge of the ranch. He managed the livestock, patrolled the fences, and maintained the houses. It was he who saw to it that whenever the son visited there was wood for the fireplace, propane for the stoves, and water coming out of the pipes.

Then the father died. The son inherited the ranch. He was now "the daddy." He was in charge. He was the one who made the decisions. The one who did the work, or made arrangements for it to be done.

The visits to the ranch of the "son-become-daddy" became more frequent, more intentional. Where once he came to get away, now he came to get things done.

Instead of walking the pastures for leisure, he now drove them in the truck, the better to carry feed and tools, or to pick up sick animals, trash, or needed rocks and wood.

Instead of looking at the beauty and wonders of nature, he now looked for threatening intruders. These could be animals such as coyotes, bobcats, or other predators. They could be noxious plant life such as mesquite, bull-nettles, or burr clover.

As he drove around the ranch, his eyes were now those of an inspector. Did the fences need repair or replacement? Was the vegetation short and sparse, time to rotate livestock to another field or pasture? Were the deer still running by this hunting blind, or did it need to be relocated?

The livestock were not watched just for entertainment. Now, he counted to see if they were all there. Or to see if neighbors' bulls had come a-visiting. How were the cattle and goats doing? Did they need doctoring? Was that calf big enough to sell? That cow or nanny past her prime and in need of replacement?

Back at the pens and houses, instead of relaxed serenity, it seemed to be a flurry of constant activity. Dirty water troughs needed cleaning. Sagging gates rehung. Leaky roofs patched. Rotting chutes replaced. Faded houses painted. Rusty pipes repaired. Root-filled sewers and drains reamed out. Empty gas tanks filled. Pestering red ant beds sprinkled with insecticide.

Even at night, instead of reading or watching TV, he now spent time keeping records, making business calls, or mulling over decisions regarding how best to take care of tomorrow's chores.

As the years passed, the "son-become-daddy" adjusted more and more to his role. But still there were times to recall how it was before. And he would wistfully long for those blissful days of yesteryear when his father was "the daddy" and he was the carefree son.

But he was mature enough, realistic enough to know this was not to be. In the continuing drama of life it was his turn to play "the daddy." So he might as well accept that role and make the most of it until his turn on the ranch stage was over and it became his son's turn to be "the daddy."

Birthdays are times of reflection for me. Time to reflect on where I am, where I've been, and where I'm going. On one of my "fifty-something" birthdays, these were a few thoughts that came to mind.

As I reflect on my faith after fifty, I feel good about where I am. It is a lot better than where I used to be.

It is better because of changing attitudes in three areas.

One is my changing attitude toward God.

I was raised on a negative image of God. God was someone out to get me for all the bad things I had done and all the good things I had not done. God was constantly keeping an account of my sins. And if that account was not settled before I died I was destined to become a permanent resident of a fiery hell for all eternity.

Needless to say, I was scared to death of God. He ranked right alongside the bogeyman on the list of people I hoped I'd never meet.

Fortunately in high school I got in with some people who had a totally different image of God. They introduced me to a God of love and mercy. A God who was a "Good Shepherd," not a "Big, Bad Wolf." A God who was for me, not against me. In short, a God I could run to. Instead of a God I would run from.

Discovering that truth has quieted my fears about God greatly. It has freed me not only from fear, but also freed me from a constant concern about my own personal salvation. Now that I know where I stand with God, I have been freed to be concerned about others.

And that is the second area of significant change in my faith — my attitude toward others.

As one who spent most of his formative years on an isolated Texas Hill Country ranch, I was raised on a goodly dose of rugged individualism. Independence and self-reliance were virtues of great value.

This held true even in the areas of religion. I thought that my faith was strictly between God and me. Phooey on everyone else!

Now, even though I still tend to be rather independent, I have discovered that I really do need other people — and that other people need me!

I have come to realize that God really knew what he was doing when he set up the church as a support group for struggling individuals. In this community of saints and sinners, this family of God, I can find comfort and joy, peace and hope, love and acceptance.

The result being that it is this sense of community, this feeling of family, that is one of the main reasons why I stay with the church.

The third area of significant change in my faith has been a changed attitude toward myself.

Again back to my upbringing. I was raised in an environment that constantly emphasized the sinful nature of humankind. Humans were basically sorry and rotten.

I heard this in church, school, and home. People were continually pointing out my weaknesses and shortcomings. And after awhile I began to believe them! I became convinced that I was a completely unacceptable sinner!

So deeply was this ingrained in me, that it became one of the most difficult things to overcome in my life.

And yet it has been overcome to a large degree, primarily because of the two things I mentioned above — my relationship to God and to other people.

When I learned that I was acceptable to God — that I was a creation of God and "God Don't Make No Junk!" — that God loved me, warts and all — this knowledge had a very positive effect upon my self-image.

And when I became aware of the significance of my relationship with other people — that a lot of people accepted me as I was, warts and all — that there were people who liked me, loved me, and needed me — this, too, gave my life meaning and purpose and, most of all, worth.

All of this finally convinced me that if I am Somebody in the eyes of God — if I am Somebody in the eyes of other people — then I can be Somebody in my own eyes, too!

That is a great feeling. I thank God, and I thank you, for giving it to me!

My thoughts about "Faith After Fifty" can be summed up in that classic statement by Martin Luther King, Jr.:

I ain't what I oughta be,
I ain't what I wanta be,
I ain't what I'm gonna be,
But, thank God, I ain't what I used to be!

ORDER FORM

Golden Goat Publishers

101 W. Mimosa
San Marcos, TX 78666

Please send me _______ copies of

YOU CAN'T WALK ON WATER IF YOU STAY IN THE BOAT by Ron Birk
at ~~$10.45~~ per book, postpaid.
$12

Please send me _______ copies of

WHAT'S A NICE GOD LIKE YOU DOING IN A PLACE LIKE THIS? by Ron Birk
at ~~$10.45~~ per book, postpaid.
$12

I have enclosed $_________.

(PLEASE PRINT)

NAME ____

ADDRESS ____

CITY ____

STATE ______________________________ ZIP ____________

FOR MORE INFORMATION CALL
512/396-0767

RON BIRK — minister, goat rancher, actor, professional speaker, writer. After 20 years as Campus Pastor at Texas A&M and Southwest Texas State Universities, Ron now works part-time as Program Director for Adult Ministry with Lutheran Outdoor & Retreat Ministries of the Southwest. The other part of his time is divided between the Texas Hill Country ranch which has been in his family for nearly 100 years and his career as a communicator. Ron has appeared as an actor in over 200 commercial and industrial videos, as well as two movies. He also speaks regularly to civic and church groups all across the country. Out of all these experiences Birk finds plenty of "RONdom Thoughts" for his weekly newspaper column.